♎

THE
LITTLE BOOK OF
SELF-CARE
— FOR —
LIBRA

*Simple Ways to Refresh
and Restore—According
to the Stars*

CONSTANCE STELLAS

ADAMS MEDIA
NEW YORK LONDON TORONTO SYDNEY NEW DELHI

Adams Media
An Imprint of Simon & Schuster, Inc.
100 Technology Center Drive
Stoughton, MA 02072

First Adams Media hardcover edition January 2019

ADAMS MEDIA and colophon are trademarks of Simon & Schuster.

For information about special discounts for bulk purchases, please contact Simon & Schuster Special Sales at 1-866-506-1949 or business@simonandschuster.com.

The Simon & Schuster Speakers Bureau can bring authors to your live event. For more information or to book an event contact the Simon & Schuster Speakers Bureau at 1-866-248-3049 or visit our website at www.simonspeakers.com.

Interior design by Colleen Cunningham
Interior images © Getty Images; Clipart.com

Manufactured in China

10 9 8 7

Library of Congress Cataloging-in-Publication Data has been applied for.

ISBN 978-1-5072-0976-9
ISBN 978-1-5072-0977-6 (ebook)

Dedication

To my social, fair-minded Libra mother, with love.

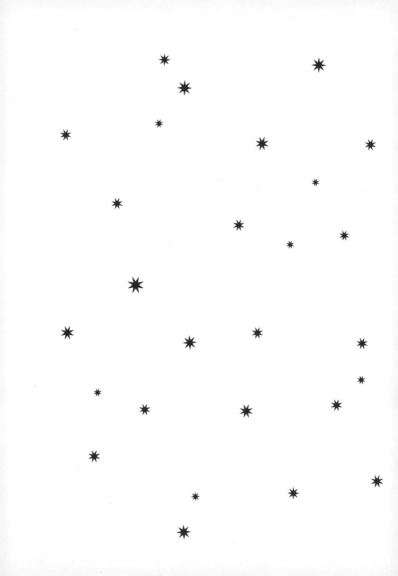

CONTENTS

Acknowledgments

I would like to thank Karen Cooper and everyone at Adams Media who helped with this book. To Brendan O'Neill, Katie Corcoran Lytle, Sarah Doughty, Eileen Mullan, Julia Jacques, Casey Ebert, Sylvia Davis, and everyone else who worked on the manuscripts. To Frank Rivera, Colleen Cunningham, and Katrina Machado for their work on the book's cover and interior design. I appreciated your team spirit and eagerness to dive into the riches of astrology.

Introduction

It's time for you to have a little *"me" time*—powered by the zodiac. By tapping into your Sun sign's astrological and elemental energies, *The Little Book of Self-Care for Libra* brings star-powered strength and cosmic relief to your life with self-care guidance tailored specifically for you.

While you may enjoy observing the world, Libra, this book focuses on your true self. This book provides information on how to incorporate self-care into your life while teaching you just how important astrology is to your overall self-care routine. You'll learn more about yourself as you learn about your sign and its governing element, air. Then you can relax, rejuvenate, and stay balanced with more than one hundred self-care ideas and activities perfect for your Libra personality.

From indulging in black cherries to opening up your living space, you will find plenty of ways to heal your mind, body, and active spirit. Now, let the stars be your self-care guide!

PART 1

SIGNS, ELEMENTS, AND SELF-CARE

CHAPTER 1

WHAT IS SELF-CARE?

✳

Astrology gives insights into whom to love, when to charge forward into new beginnings, and how to succeed in whatever you put your mind to. When paired with self-care, astrology can also help you relax and reclaim that part of yourself that tends to get lost in the bustle of the day. In this chapter you'll learn what self-care is—for you. (No matter your sign, self-care is more than just lit candles and quiet reflection, though these activities may certainly help you find the renewal that you seek.) You'll also learn how making a priority of personalized self-care activities can benefit you in ways you may not even have thought of. Whether you're a Libra, a Pisces, or a Taurus, you deserve rejuvenation and renewal that's customized to your sign—this chapter reveals where to begin.

What Self-Care Is

Self-care is any activity that you do to take care of yourself. It rejuvenates your body, refreshes your mind, or realigns your spirit. It relaxes and refuels you. It gets you ready for a new day or a fresh start. It's the practices, rituals, and meaningful activities that you do, just for you, that help you feel safe, grounded, happy, and fulfilled.

The activities that qualify as self-care are amazingly unique and personalized to who you are, what you like, and, in large part, what your astrological sign is. If you're asking questions about what self-care practices are best for those ruled by air and born under the diplomatic eye of Libra, you'll find answers—and restoration—in Part 2. But, no matter which of those self-care activities speak to you and your unique place in the universe on any given day, it will fall into one of the following self-care categories—each of which pertains to a different aspect of your life:

* Physical self-care
* Emotional self-care
* Social self-care
* Mental self-care
* Spiritual self-care
* Practical self-care

When you practice all of these unique types of self-care—and prioritize your practice to ensure you are choosing the best options for your unique sign and governing element—know that you are actively working to create the version of yourself that the universe intends you to be.

Physical Self-Care

When you practice physical self-care, you make the decision to look after and restore the one physical body that has been bestowed upon you. Care for it. Use it in the best way you can imagine, for that is what the universe wishes you to do. You can't light the world on fire or move mountains if you're not doing everything you can to take care of your physical health.

Emotional Self-Care

Emotional self-care is when you take the time to acknowledge and care for your inner self, your emotional well-being. Whether you're angry or frustrated, happy or joyful, or somewhere in between, emotional self-care happens when you choose to sit with your emotions: when you step away from the noise of daily life that often drowns out or tamps down your authentic self. Emotional self-care lets you see your inner you as the cosmos intend. Once you identify your true emotions, you can either accept them and continue to move forward on your journey or you can try to change any negative emotions for the better. The more you acknowledge your feelings and practice emotional self-care, the more you'll feel the positivity that the universe and your life holds for you.

Social Self-Care

You practice social self-care when you nurture your relationships with others, be they friends, coworkers, or family members. In today's hectic world it's easy to let relationships fall to the wayside, but it's so important to share your life with others—and let others share their lives with you. Social self-care is reciprocal and often karmic. The support and love that you put out into the universe through social self-care is given back to you by those you socialize with—often tenfold.

Mental Self-Care

Mental self-care is anything that keeps your mind working quickly and critically. It helps you cut through the fog of the day, week, or year and ensures that your quick wit and sharp mind are intact and working the way the cosmos intended. Making sure your mind is fit helps you problem-solve, decreases stress since you're not feeling overwhelmed, and keeps you feeling on top of your mental game—no matter your sign or your situation.

Spiritual Self-Care

Spiritual self-care is self-care that allows you to tap into your soul and the soul of the universe and uncover its secrets. Rather than focusing on a particular religion or set of religious beliefs, these types of self-care activities reconnect you with a higher power: the sense that something out there is bigger than you. When you meditate, you connect. When you pray, you connect. Whenever you do something that allows you to experience and marry yourself to the vastness that is the cosmos, you practice spiritual self-care.

Practical Self-Care

Self-care is what you do to take care of yourself, and practical self-care, while not as expansive as the other types, is made up of the seemingly small day-to-day tasks that bring you peace and accomplishment. These practical self-care rituals are important, but are often overlooked. Scheduling a doctor's appointment that you've been putting off is practical self-care. Getting your hair cut is practical self-care. Anything you can check off your list of things to be accomplished gives you a sacred space to breathe and allows the universe more room to bring a beautiful sense of cosmic fulfillment your way.

What Self-Care Isn't

Self-care is restorative. Self-care is clarifying. Self-care is whatever you need to do to make yourself feel secure in the universe.

Now that you know what self-care is, it's also important that you're able to see what self-care isn't. Self-care is not something that you force yourself to do because you think it will be good for you. Some signs are energy in motion and sitting still goes against their place in the universe. Those signs won't feel refreshed by lying in a hammock or sitting down to meditate. Other signs aren't able to ground themselves unless they've found a self-care practice that protects their cosmic need for peace and quiet. Those signs won't find parties, concerts, and loud venues soothing or satisfying. If a certain ritual doesn't bring you peace, clarity, or satisfaction, then it's not right for your sign and you should find something that speaks to you more clearly.

There's a difference though between not finding satisfaction in a ritual that you've tried and not wanting to try a self-care activity because you're tired or stuck in a comfort zone. Sometimes going to the gym or meeting up with friends is the self-care practice that you need to experience—whether engaging in it feels like a downer or not. So consider how you feel when you're actually doing the activity. If it feels invigorating to get on the treadmill or you feel delight when you actually catch up with your friend, the ritual is doing what it should be doing and clearing space for you—among other benefits...

The Benefits of Self-Care

The benefits of self-care are boundless and there's none that's superior to helping you put rituals in place to feel more at home in your body, in your spirit, and in your unique home in the cosmos. There are, however, other benefits to engaging in the practice of self-care that you should know.

Rejuvenates Your Immune System

No matter which rituals are designated for you by the stars, your sign, and its governing element, self-care helps both your body and mind rest, relax, and recuperate. The practice of self-care activates the parasympathetic nervous system (often called the rest and digest system), which slows your heart rate, calms the body, and overall helps your body relax and release tension. This act of decompression gives your body the space it needs to build up and strengthen your immune system, which protects you from illness.

Helps You Reconnect—with Yourself

When you practice the ritual of self-care—especially when you customize this practice based on your personal sign and governing element—you learn what you like to do and what you need to do to replenish yourself. Knowing yourself better, and allowing yourself the time and space that you need to focus on your personal needs and desires, gives you the gifts of self-confidence and self-knowledge. Setting time aside to focus on your needs also helps you put busy, must-do things aside, which gives you time to reconnect with yourself and who you are deep inside.

Increases Compassion

Perhaps one of the most important benefits of creating a self-care ritual is that, by focusing on yourself, you become more compassionate to others as well. When you truly take the time to care for yourself and make yourself and your importance in the universe a priority in your own life, you're then able to care for others and see their needs and desires in a new way. You can't pour from an empty dipper, and self-care allows you the space and clarity to do what you can to send compassion out into the world.

Starting a Self-Care Routine

Self-care should be treated as a ritual in your life, something you make the time to pause for, no matter what. You are important. You deserve rejuvenation and a sense of relaxation. You need to open your soul to the gifts that the universe is giving you, and self-care provides you with a way to ensure you're ready to receive those gifts. To begin a self-care routine, start by making yourself the priority. Do the customized rituals in Part 2 with intention, knowing the universe has already given them to you, by virtue of your sign and your governing element.

Now that you understand the role that self-care will hold in your life, let's take a closer look at the connection between self-care and astrology.

CHAPTER 2

SELF-CARE
AND ASTROLOGY

✴

A strology is the study of the connection between the objects in the heavens (the planets,
the stars) and what happens here on earth. Just as
the movements of the planets and other heavenly
bodies influence the ebb and flow of the tides, so
do they influence you—your body, your mind, your
spirit. This relationship is ever present and is never
more important—or personal—than when viewed
through the lens of self-care.

In this chapter you'll learn how the locations of these celestial bodies at the time of your birth affect you and define the self-care activities that will speak directly to you as a Leo, an Aries, a Capricorn, or any of the other zodiac signs. You'll see how the zodiac influences every part of your being and why ignoring its lessons can leave you feeling frustrated and unfulfilled. You'll also realize that, when you perform the rituals of self-care based on your sign, the wisdom of the cosmos will lead you down a path of fulfillment and restoration—to the return of who *you* really are, deep inside.

Zodiac Polarities

In astrology, all signs are mirrored by other signs that are on the opposite side of the zodiac. This polarity ensures that the zodiac is balanced and continues to flow with an unbreakable, even stream of energy. There are two different polarities in the zodiac and each is called by a number of different names:

* Yang/masculine/positive polarity
* Yin/feminine/negative polarity

Each polar opposite embodies a number of opposing traits, qualities, and attributes that will influence which self-care practices will work for or against your sign and your own personal sense of cosmic balance.

Yang

Whether male or female, those who fall under yang, or masculine, signs are extroverted and radiate their energy outward. They are spontaneous, active, bold, and fearless. They move forward in life with the desire to enjoy everything the world has to offer to them, and they work hard to transfer their inspiration and positivity to others so that those individuals may experience the same gifts that the universe offers them. All signs governed by the fire and air elements are yang and hold the potential for these dominant qualities. We will refer to them with masculine pronouns. These signs are:

* Aries
* Leo
* Sagittarius
* Gemini
* Libra
* Aquarius

There are people who hold yang energy who are introverted and retiring. However, by practicing self-care that is customized for your sign and understanding the potential ways to use your energy, you can find a way—perhaps one that's unique to you—to claim your native buoyancy and dominance and engage with the path that the universe opens for you.

Yin

Whether male or female, those who fall under yin, or feminine, signs are introverted and radiate inwardly. They draw people and experiences to them rather than seeking people and experiences in an extroverted way. They move forward in life with an energy that is reflective, receptive, and focused on communication and achieving shared goals. All signs governed by the earth and water elements are yin and hold the potential for these reflective qualities. We will refer to them with feminine pronouns. These signs are:

* Taurus
* Virgo
* Capricorn
* Cancer
* Scorpio
* Pisces

As there are people with yang energy who are introverted and retiring, there are also people with yin energy who are outgoing and extroverted. And by practicing self-care rituals that speak to your particular sign, energy, and governing body, you will reveal your true self and the balance of energy will be maintained.

Governing Elements

Each astrological sign has a governing element that defines their energy orientation and influences both the way the sign moves through the universe and relates to self-care. The elements are fire, earth, air, and water. All the signs in each element share certain characteristics, along with having their own sign-specific qualities:

* **Fire:** Fire signs are adventurous, bold, and energetic. They enjoy the heat and warm environments and look to the sun and fire as a means to recharge their depleted batteries. They're competitive, outgoing, and passionate. The fire signs are Aries, Leo, and Sagittarius.
* **Earth:** Earth signs all share a common love and tendency toward a practical, material, sensual, and economic orientation. The earth signs are Taurus, Virgo, and Capricorn.
* **Air:** Air is the most ephemeral element and those born under this element are thinkers, innovators, and communicators. The air signs are Gemini, Libra, and Aquarius.
* **Water:** Water signs are instinctual, compassionate, sensitive, and emotional. The water signs are Cancer, Scorpio, and Pisces.

Chapter 3 teaches you all about the ways your specific governing element influences and drives your connection to your cosmically harmonious self-care rituals, but it's important that you realize how important these elemental traits are to your self-care practice and to the activities that will help restore and reveal your true self.

Sign Qualities

Each of the astrological elements governs three signs. Each of these three signs is also given its own quality or mode, which corresponds to a different part of each season: the beginning, the middle, or the end.

* **Cardinal signs:** The cardinal signs initiate and lead in each season. Like something that is just starting out, they are actionable, enterprising, and assertive, and are born leaders. The cardinal signs are Aries, Cancer, Libra, and Capricorn.
* **Fixed signs:** The fixed signs come into play when the season is well established. They are definite, consistent, reliable, motivated by principles, and powerfully stubborn. The fixed signs are Taurus, Leo, Scorpio, and Aquarius.
* **Mutable signs:** The mutable signs come to the forefront when the seasons are changing. They are part of one season, but also part of the next. They are adaptable, versatile, and flexible. The mutable signs are Gemini, Virgo, Sagittarius, and Pisces.

Each of these qualities tells you a lot about yourself and who you are. They also give you invaluable information about the types of self-care rituals that your sign will find the most intuitive and helpful.

Ruling Planets

In addition to qualities and elements, each specific sign is ruled by a particular planet that lends its personality to those born under that sign. Again, these sign-specific traits give you valuable insight into the personality of the signs and the self-care rituals that may best rejuvenate them. The signs that correspond to each planet—and the ways that those planetary influences determine your self-care options—are as follows:

* **Aries:** Ruled by Mars, Aries is passionate, energetic, and determined.
* **Taurus:** Ruled by Venus, Taurus is sensual, romantic, and fertile.
* **Gemini:** Ruled by Mercury, Gemini is intellectual, changeable, and talkative.
* **Cancer:** Ruled by the Moon, Cancer is nostalgic, emotional, and home loving.
* **Leo:** Ruled by the Sun, Leo is fiery, dramatic, and confident.
* **Virgo:** Ruled by Mercury, Virgo is intellectual, analytical, and responsive.
* **Libra:** Ruled by Venus, Libra is beautiful, romantic, and graceful.
* **Scorpio:** Ruled by Mars and Pluto, Scorpio is intense, powerful, and magnetic.
* **Sagittarius:** Ruled by Jupiter, Sagittarius is optimistic, boundless, and larger than life.

* **Capricorn:** Ruled by Saturn, Capricorn is wise, patient, and disciplined.
* **Aquarius:** Ruled by Uranus, Aquarius is independent, unique, and eccentric.
* **Pisces:** Ruled by Neptune and Jupiter, Pisces is dreamy, sympathetic, and idealistic.

A Word on Sun Signs

When someone is a Leo, Aries, Sagittarius, or any of the other zodiac signs, it means that the sun was positioned in this constellation in the heavens when they were born. Your Sun sign is a dominant factor in defining your personality, your best self-care practices, and your soul nature. Every person also has the position of the Moon, Mercury, Venus, Mars, Jupiter, Saturn, Uranus, Neptune, and Pluto. These planets can be in any of the elements: fire signs, earth signs, air signs, or water signs. If you have your entire chart calculated by an astrologer or on an Internet site, you can see the whole picture and learn about all your elements. Someone born under Leo with many signs in another element will not be as concentrated in the fire element as someone with five or six planets in Leo. Someone born in Pisces with many signs in another element will not be as concentrated in the water element as someone with five or six planets in Pisces. And so on. Astrology is a complex system and has many shades of meaning. For our purposes, looking at the self-care practices designated by your Sun sign, or what most people consider *their* sign, will give you the information you need to move forward and find fulfillment and restoration.

CHAPTER 3

ESSENTIAL ELEMENTS: AIR

✳

The air element is perhaps the most elusive element of the zodiac. Air is everywhere—invisible, and yet completely necessary for life. We are so sensitive to air that we even feel a momentary change in the currents around us or the amount of oxygen in our body.

In astrology, air is the third element of creation, preceded by earth and fire. The air signs (Gemini, Libra, and Aquarius) are the thinkers of the zodiac. Their dominion is mental—the realm of ideas and concepts. For example, you may have heard the saying that a person "builds castles in the air" or "has his head in the clouds." These statements are usually made as pejorative expressions, but for air signs they describe the essence of who they are. Air signs live in a world of both rational and intuitive thought. They are imaginative and dream, sometimes idealistically, of new and better ways to be, to think, and to communicate. Any self-care they do must reflect that disposition as well. Let's take a look at the mythological importance of air and its counterparts, the basic characteristics of the three air signs, and what they all have in common when it comes to self-care.

The Mythology of Air

In Greek mythology the legend of Icarus has a symbolic meaning with the air element. In this myth Icarus and his father, Daedalus, a talented Athenian craftsman responsible for building a labyrinth for King Minos to imprison the Minotaur, were themselves imprisoned in the labyrinth in Crete for crimes against the king. To escape the Minotaur, Daedalus fashioned wings of wax and feathers that he and his son could use to fly over the sea. Daedalus warned his son not to fly too near the sun as the heat would cause his wings to melt. But Icarus became enchanted by his freedom and flew too close to the sun. Soon, the wax melted and Icarus fell into the sea.

The lesson for the air signs in this myth is that going beyond sense and reason usually does not work out. In the case of Icarus, he followed his desire instead of his rational side, and ended up falling to his death. Ideas are wonderful—they are the foundation of many great creations. But for air signs, ideas are followed by the hard work of grounding them in physical reality. Self-care rituals that cater to both mind and heart are key for air signs, but balance and rationale are often paramount.

The Element of Air

Air signs are known for their curiosity, pursuit of knowledge, and keen ability to communicate. They delight in conversation and feel most passionate when they are confronting a dilemma of the mind straight on. But their grand ideas sometimes make them unpredictable. Because of this, they must be challenged in all parts of their lives. Doing the same thing over and over will just leave them bored. This goes for self-care as well. They need variety and different options for wellness activities, or they may not participate at all. Air signs are buoyant, perceptive, and inventive. For example, Gemini is expressive and always ready to entertain. Libra is gentle and will listen to a friend's troubles for hours. And Aquarius is ingenious, helping to solve problems with different approaches.

Astrological Symbols

The astrological symbols (also called the zodiacal symbols) of the air signs also give you hints as to how air signs move through the world. Each symbol ties back to the analytical, curious nature associated with air signs:

* Gemini is the Twins
* Libra is the Scales
* Aquarius is the Water Bearer

All these signs show intimate harmony with the cycles of the seasons and a personal connection with air. Gemini represents duality of the mind, and his symbol resembles the Roman numeral two. Libra brings balance with his scales of justice. And Aquarius represents positive movement and nourishment with waves of water or electricity. Each air sign's personality and subsequent approaches to self-care tie back to the qualities of these symbols.

Signs and Seasonal Modes

Each of the elements in astrology has a sign that corresponds to a different part of each season.

* **Fixed:** Aquarius is a fixed air sign. He rules in winter. The fixed signs are definite, motivated by principles, and powerfully stubborn.
* **Mutable:** Gemini is the first air sign and marks the end of spring and the beginning of summer. Gemini is called a mutable air sign because he ushers us from one season to the next. Mutable signs are changeable and flexible.
* **Cardinal:** Libra, the second air sign, occurs in autumn; he is the cardinal air sign because the autumn equinox occurs around Libra's time. The cardinal signs are leaders and action-oriented.

If you know your element and whether you are a cardinal, fixed, or mutable sign, you know a lot about yourself. This is invaluable for self-care and is reflected in the customized air sign self-care rituals found in Part 2.

Air Signs and Self-Care

When it comes to self-care, air signs must realize that they have a very sensitive nervous system. Not only do they react to changes in the weather and the "vibrations" around them in social situations, they also react to the power of words and ideas. Sometimes, they are not aware that their words can wound others, but they are always aware when someone says something hurtful to them. However, air signs are not a feeling sign, they are a thinking sign. They perceive that they are angry or hurt, but their feelings are expressed more in terms of the other person's actions, so they'll respond with "I thought that was rude," or "how unkind and cruel." Self-care must involve tapping into their emotions as well as the logic that precedes them.

Air signs are not oriented toward the physical. For instance, they know they have to eat and take care of their health, but the action comes second to thinking about it all. They can lose track of time and forget that they only had a croissant for breakfast! The first part of any self-care program for air signs is to understand the concept that self-care is a good thing to do for an easier and more productive life. Long-range thinking is an air sign specialty, so why not apply it to long-range self-care goals? This makes intuitive sense to air signs. In this way the most successful self-care activities should be interesting and involve an overall concept, such as "If I do this, I will learn some new ways of understanding myself and others," or "This is a new therapy that promises to eliminate my posture problem. I will check it out." Just doing something is not enough—air signs want to be sure of their reasons.

Repeating meaningless habits is a pitfall for air signs. If they get stuck in a rut, they'll ditch their self-care and run off to a party instead. Air signs are creative, and the same effort they exert for a nice dinner, social outing, story, or song should also apply to self-care. On the flip side, any activity or program that is cumbersome won't last long with air signs. If there is too much equipment to deal with or too much effort to get to that particular gym or hiking trail, the air sign just won't do it.

Air signs have an aesthetic sense in all aspects of their lives, which is why any self-care activity has to be effective as well as pleasing to the eye. For example, a diet plan must be tasty and involve food that is beautifully displayed. Those two qualities please air signs and will motivate them. The plan also has to be simple to follow. No elaborate timetables, just clear directions.

So now that you know what air signs need to practice self-care, let's look at each of the balanced characteristics of Libra and how he can maintain his gifts.

CHAPTER 4
SELF-CARE FOR LIBRA

✳

Dates: September 23–October 22
Element: Air
Polarity: Yang
Quality: Cardinal
Symbol: Scales
Ruler: Venus

Libra is the second air sign of the zodiac. He is yang and a cardinal sign and begins around the autumn equinox when the day and night are in perfect balance. Libra also marks the beginning of the soul's journey toward relationships. The word *we* comes to Libra's lips more easily than *I*, as he thinks of life in terms of relationships and sometimes in his zeal assumes that his personal preferences are always enjoyable to his partners.

Libra's goal is to balance *we* and *me*. Libra can become unbalanced because he sees all sides of every issue and everyone's opinion. He considers too many possibilities. This leads to conflicts of opinion within himself.

Libra's symbol is the Scales, and he is the only sign of the zodiac whose symbol is an inanimate object. Libra can sometimes be detached and superior to the chaotic feelings of other people as he weighs all thoughts. At its best, this tendency gives him a great ability to judge fairly and fight for equality between people. At its worst, it makes Libra aloof and condescending toward others.

The planet Venus is Libra's ruler. In Roman mythology Venus (known as Aphrodite in Greek mythology) was the goddess who beguiled men and gods alike. The Romans believed that she brought laughter and love to the mortal world. Other myths state that Venus was treacherous and malicious and exerted a deadly destructive power over men. The two parts of the Libran personality are described in these myths: the gracious partner who shares his joy with everyone, and the heartbreaker. Libra spends his life balancing these extremes.

There is grit and determination beneath the charm and smiles in both Libran women and men. In fact, Libra is often called the steel hand in the velvet glove. Additionally, the female Venus and male yang within Libra provide a balance of feminine and masculine traits. Libran women can be very tough and politically minded, and Libran men often have an eye for aesthetics.

Self-Care and Libra

Libra understands himself through his relationships. In his quest to keep the peace, he can become very involved in figuring out the best strategies for achieving personal and communal goals and avoiding conflict—and Libra does *not* like conflict. Charming and full of grand ideas, he frequently stirs things up, but learns over time how to quell any high winds that may blow. The best self-care for him includes fresh air to calm his constant whirl of thoughts.

Since relationships are so important to Libra, he frequently needs time to himself to find his center, which can become lost in all of his generosity and focus on others. Finding this center requires checking in with the way he feels about things, rather than concentrating on what he thinks. Feeling does not come naturally, as Libra is a thinking sign. When Libra talks about something important, he will say "I think this," rather than "I feel this." He wants to get down to the concrete reasons for his reactions. Taking a time-out throughout the day to see if the Scales are tipping or are balanced will lead Libra in good directions for all of his self-care practices. Libra responds best to self-care that involves both mental and physical practices. As a positive yang sign, Libra is naturally an optimistic thinker. When something is not working out in his life, he can change his thought patterns easily to reevaluate what adjustments he can make to be successful.

When Libra is unable to reframe his mind-set or needs a little help in sorting out all of his whirling thoughts, he benefits from counseling and therapy. Libra wants to understand his psyche, so he needs someone with wisdom and patience who will help guide him through his many thoughts and questions. Libra already has dozens of relationships that require his time and energy, so if the therapist is too chummy and reveals too much of their personal life, it will not help him. Instead of exploring his own identity, Libra will be focused on what the therapist thinks of him. Once he finds the right therapist, Libra will commit to counseling for a long time.

The best physical self-care for Libra involves toning exercises that improve his strength and posture without leaving him feeling sweaty and unkempt.

A motivating factor in exercising is what Libra wears. No ratty T-shirts here: colorful and well-fitting exercise garb is a must. While Libra can give his all to a workout, he likes to make sure he looks good doing it.

Libra Rules the Kidneys

Libra rules over the kidneys, so self-care that focuses on this part of the body is especially important. In practical terms Libra should take care that his lower back area is always warm. After swimming, he should change to avoid sitting in wet, damp clothes. Drinking enough water is also very important, as it keeps the kidneys functioning properly. It can be hard to monitor care of your kidneys because they are internal organs, but Libra should be mindful of any kidney or bladder disturbances and have a doctor check them out.

Libra's rulership of the kidneys has both a physical and symbolic meaning. Physically, the kidneys purify the body, removing waste and moving clean blood up to the heart. In the psychological and spiritual realm, Libra's mission is to purify consciousness through his relationships and just decisions. Libra understands that through peace and balance the world will thrive.

Libra and Self-Care Success

A motivating factor for Libra in self-care is vanity! Libra likes to look good and will work hard to achieve that goal. Ideas about balance are all well and good, but when the reflection in the mirror looks healthy and well rested, Libra feels good. Sports that interest Libra have a touch of elegance about them. Tennis, golf, and ballet are activities that Libra will enjoy. Libra has a great deal of physical grace and enjoys fluid movement. However, there is hidden aggression in Libra that he is usually too polite to express. Graceful sports that give him an outlet for this pent-up energy include martial arts such as aikido, tai chi, and kendo.

Libra is also very involved with how other people react to him, and when he sees that something he is doing brings good attention and compliments, he will keep it up. The flip side of Libra's social nature—and a pitfall to good self-care—is too much socializing. This, coupled with his desire to impress, can lead to overindulgence with food, drink, and late nights. Because he wants the feeling of comradery and friendship, he can easily be swayed by the crowd—staying that hour or two more, having that additional drink. Before long, Libra is running on fumes. It may be boring to be mindful of balancing work, play, and obligations, but moderation is essential to Libra's success in self-care.

Another important element of Libra's self-care is sleep. If illness or agitation interrupts his sleep cycle, Libra wakes up feeling unbalanced. Sleep aids such as meditation tapes, stretching before bed, a glass of warm milk, or breathing exercises can help. And as soon as Libra is back in a proper sleep cycle, he feels in balance and in control of his thoughts.

Symbolized by the Scales, Libra values fairness for others and himself. While it is easy for Libra to be fair to others, he is learning to care for himself, and this skill will be a key to his success in overall self-care. When he is fair to himself, it makes the Libran Scales shine, and when he strikes a balance between others and the self, and justice and forgiveness, he gives his gifts of kindness, equilibrium, and joy to all. And there is no better way to keep the Scales balanced than by taking care of your Libran needs. So let's take a look at some self-care activities especially designed for you, Libra.

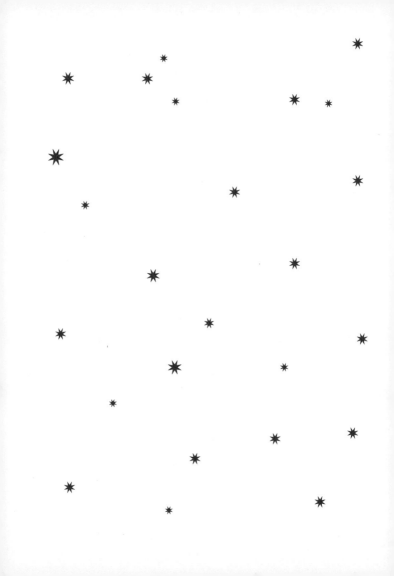

PART 2

SELF-CARE
RITUALS
— FOR —
LIBRA

Go Cloud-Watching

——————————

Air signs are intellectual thinkers who excel at creative thought and problem-solving. But sometimes that can mean it's hard to turn off your racing thoughts. If you're having trouble figuring out the answer to a question, take care of yourself today by taking a well-deserved break to clear your mind. Need something else to focus on? Look up at the clouds. Take some time to lie back and watch the clouds move through the sky. You're sure to feel refreshed and will be able to look at any challenges with a fresh perspective.

Smile

_____

Spreading joy is one of charming Libra's not-so-secret talents. Practice that Libran smile, even when things may not be going your way. Smile at your neighbors as you leave for work, and strangers you pass during your day. Even treat that less-than-pleasant cashier to a smile. You never know what someone may be dealing with in their personal life, so rather than see their curtness as an affront that deserves a similar reaction, stay positive and smiling. Who knows, you may just brighten someone's day!

Head to the Swimming Pool

_____

I t may come as a surprise, but swimming is actually great for air signs. Air signs are known for loving to think about problems from every angle, but sometimes it's important to have a mental break. With swimming you'll need to focus on mastering each movement and maintaining fluid motions, so it's a great way to calm your mind. Allow yourself to relax and feel restored as you take a break from your worries.

Swimming is also a great way for air signs to get some exercise. Regular swim sessions will help you build lung power and stamina. So instead of your regular workout, head to your local pool and do some laps.

Give Your Décor a Luxe Touch

Ruled by Venus, Libra cannot abide ugly surroundings. All décor in his home or office should have a touch of luxury and beauty—both treasured elements of his ruling planet. Art Deco furniture especially appeals to Libra, as it evokes a sense of harmony and symmetry. Be sure to balance all pictures so they are symmetrical and the colors don't clash! Accents in shades of green will add an extra touch of balance and overall tranquility to your space.

Indulge in Dark Chocolate

As a sign ruled by sensual Venus, Libra has quite the sweet tooth. Dark chocolate is the perfect treat when you find yourself longing for something sweet. Dark chocolate is also richer than milk chocolate and has less processed sugar, so you'll need less to get your fill—not to mention dark chocolate boasts a number of health-giving qualities, including tons of antioxidants. It can also help reduce blood pressure, improve brain function, and reduce the risk of heart disease!

Use Writing Prompts

A ir signs are often creative and great at expression. Why not try channeling those skills into some writing? Some well-known authors such as Shel Silverstein, Oscar Wilde, Charles Dickens, and Judy Blume were able to channel their air sign qualities into incredible literary works—maybe you can too!

Not sure where to start? Writing prompts are a great way to boost your creativity and give you the kind of challenge you love. Look for a writing prompt book at your local library, or check out different social media communities for ideas to help you get started.

Unplug Before Bed

Even the most communicative air sign will
sometimes need a break to feel refreshed and
reenergized after a long day. Getting a good night's
sleep will also help rejuvenate your nervous system,
so do whatever you can to ensure pleasant dreams
and a restful evening.

A good first step is to unplug from social media
before heading to bed, and, if possible, keep technology out of the bedroom entirely. Stop scrolling
through social media and give yourself a break from
your tablet or computer. Minimize your information
input by avoiding TV—especially news programs—
before bedtime. If possible you can even eliminate
clocks from your bedroom for a more peaceful sleep.

Invest in Copperware

Venus, the celestial matriarch of Libra, rules copper. Its lustrous color makes a great decoration, which classy Libra will appreciate. And it is also a useful addition to your kitchen! Copper pots and pans allow you to easily change and control the heat of your food as it cooks.

Copper also promotes balance. According to Ayurveda theory, occasionally using a copper vessel to drink water from can balance your doshas (the three energies that are believed to make up your being). Similar to the five classical elements, the three doshas of Pitta (fire and water), Vata (air and space), and Kapha (water and earth) influence your behavior, and each energy relies on the others to strike a healthy balance. Has your fiery Pitta energy taken the reins lately? Sip cold water from a copper mug to harmonize it with your other energies.

Whistle Your Way Through Chores

Vacuuming or washing dishes might not be your favorite activity, but sometimes those boring chores simply need to get done. Intellectual air signs need some kind of fun activity to keep the mind otherwise occupied, especially when faced with a few hours of dusting and sweeping. Try whistling or humming while doing chores. It'll help keep your brain focused as you work, and may be a good creative outlet if you're especially interested in music. You'll also help strengthen your lungs—all that humming is a mini-breathing exercise!

Pay Someone a Compliment

Friendly Libra compliments freely and doesn't mind receiving a compliment—or two or three—himself. Cultivating connections with people, even if just for a moment as you pass a coworker in the hallway or hug a friend goodbye, delights Libra's outgoing and sociable nature.

Try to compliment not just outward appearance, but also character traits you admire. While "I love your shoes" is very flattering, "You are such a great listener" will stay with the person you compliment for a long time. You may just get some flattery in return, though sparking a positive connection to that person will be reward enough.

Create the Perfect Work Space

Air signs are intellectual problem-solvers with great critical-thinking skills. Make sure your work space is ready! Whether you work at home or spend your days in a professional office, it's important to make sure you create a productive work space. Start with your chair so you're comfortable and able to focus. Your chair should be lightweight and on rollers so you can move around easily. Your spontaneous nature will appreciate the ease with which you can shift around and collaborate with your coworkers.

If you work around a lot of computers and technical equipment, ask an expert about setting up a portable ionizer to help neutralize their electromagnetic vibrations. It will help improve the air quality and keep you feeling your best.

Treasure Your Keepsakes

R uled by Venus, Libra is a romantic at heart, fond
of revisiting memories time and time again. One
great way to relive favorite memories is by keeping
a collection of mementos that you can pull out and
sift through whenever you want. Use a treasure chest
to store all of your special keepsakes. When you are
feeling less than your upbeat self, you can take out
your "treasure" for an uplifting trip down memory
lane. Look for a chest with sophisticated accents or
an elegant wood finish to delight your aesthetic side.

Eat Black Cherries

Boasting a sweet flavor and rich color, black cherries should be the mascot for Libra's sensual ruling planet, Venus. Not only are they a delightful treat, but they are also quite healthful! A compound in black cherries helps prevent inflammation and premature aging by fighting free radicals that can cause inflamed tissue and cell damage. Cherries also contain melatonin, a natural relaxant that will help ever-active Libra go to sleep.

How can you not feel posh reclining on your sofa with a bowl of cherries? Venus approves of this sensual act of self-care.

Learn about Aikido

_____

Inspired by various martial arts techniques, aikido is more than fighting—it's really about self-development, focus, peace, and balance. Participants can use their practice to find what they need, whether that's a healthy workout or a focus on spirituality. To get started, look for beginners' classes in your area or check on online course offerings for a better idea of what to expect before signing up.

Perfect for air signs, aikido is a powerful and beautiful martial art. Since air signs may enjoy opportunities for self-improvement and collaboration, aikido can be a great way to focus your overactive mind on yourself. You'll appreciate the graceful movements that will remind you of your air-like qualities.

Become a Social Butterfly

Connection is your strong suit, so head out to events, get-togethers, and parties to meet new people. Social events bring out the best in air signs, who are in their element when surrounded by engaging conversation and interesting ideas. Try attending a reading at your local bookstore, checking out the speakers at a nearby college, or simply following your friends to a party. Socializing with different types of people comes naturally to air signs, so you may find your friend group growing rapidly in ways you never expected. You'll increase your own knowledge of the world by meeting other people, so don't be afraid to let your natural social butterfly tendencies shine!

Snack on Almonds

Almonds aren't just a tasty snack! They also contain tons of antioxidants that lower blood pressure, curb hunger, and maintain healthy kidney function. Healthy kidneys are especially important to Libran wellness, as they are the part of the body that he rules. Your kidneys remove toxins and other waste from your blood and send the purified blood back up to your heart. They also release erythropoietin, a hormone that stimulates the production of red blood cells; renin, an enzyme that regulates your blood pressure; and active vitamin D, which maintains calcium levels for healthy bone growth. (If you suffer from kidney disease, check with your doctor to see if almonds are beneficial for you.)

Almonds are an easy snack to take on-the-go, so be sure to slip a packet into your bag before you head out for that next social gathering.

Record Your Ideas

A ir signs are creative and often have a lot of ideas. Those ideas may be interesting and worth exploring in more detail, but they can sometimes require a little more thought than you're able to give in the moment. So give yourself an outlet to brainstorm and release those ideas in a constructive manner by writing everything down and keeping a record of your ideas—no matter how big or small they seem. You may consider keeping a journal and taking some time every day to record your thoughts, or you may just want to jot down your notes on your smartphone as they come to you.

Keep an eye out for patterns in your thinking—they might help reveal worries or build on broader ideas you didn't even realize you had.

Display Your Totem

Libra is symbolized by the balance scale, an ancient tool of measure featuring two bowls suspended from a support beam. Display a small brass spice scale on your desk or in your living space. This Libran totem will serve as a reminder of the essential balance in life. If you are having trouble finding harmony or working out what is right in a particular situation, look to your scale for inspiration and a boost of confidence. Try balancing out objects in the scale to symbolize your ability to always find an equilibrium.

Get Some Fresh Air

H ere's an easy way for air signs to take care of themselves: head outside to get some fresh air! Air signs truly value freedom and openness, so make sure to break up your day by spending some time outside. Take your morning coffee out to your porch, enjoy a book outside, or spend some time outdoors during the evenings and weekends. Choose to walk instead of drive wherever possible—not only will you feel healthier and more refreshed, but the environment will thank you as well!

"Vitamin O"—oxygen—is one of the most important things to keep an air sign feeling revitalized and healthy.

Enjoy a Relaxing Bath

As a sign ruled by Venus, Libra enjoys the sensual experience of a warm bath. Create a relaxing space for your bath with sweet-smelling candles, lots of bubble bath, and music turned to a low volume. Waltz rhythms are a sophisticated and calming choice. Try "The Blue Danube," a classic by Johann Strauss II; you may recognize it from popular films such as *Titanic* and *2001: A Space Odyssey*.

This elegant, pampering act of self-care will leave you feeling renewed and ready for whatever is in store—whether it's an outing with friends, or bedtime.

Support Clean Air

The environment is important to everyone, and air pollution is a cause any air sign can really get behind. It's important to take care of your health, and air signs will instinctually gravitate toward clean air as a way to keep their bodies strong, healthy, and happy.

Get involved in the movement for clean air! Do some research to learn about particular causes you'd like to support, like wind farms or other alternative energies. Donate to major clean air groups to help them fund their important work. Find out what programs exist in your area where you can volunteer your time. Air signs are great communicators, so volunteer your skills to help get the word out on clean air!

Keep In Touch with Friends

A ir signs are great at intercommunication, and it's important for their well-being to have that social interaction throughout their lives. Other signs though? Not so much. Before you get upset that you haven't heard from your friends in a while, try making the first move and reaching out. Send a quick text to a friend you haven't heard from in a while. Give your best friend a call, even if you only want to say hello. Reconnect with old friends over social media, or even send an email to let someone know you're thinking of them.

With our busy lives, people sometimes need reminders to keep in touch, and air signs are the perfect ones to take that step!

Treat Yourself to Silk Pajamas

Venus, Libra's sensual ruling planet, is in charge of all plush textures, including silk. Invest in a pair of silk pajamas. This cool, smooth fabric feels heavenly on your skin—and it's impossible to not feel fabulous in it. The soothing effect of silk will also help you slip into dreamland, which can be difficult for airy Libra, whose mind is always busily swirling through the clouds. Look for pajamas in light pink or deep blue shades, as these colors promote serenity and restful sleep.

Learn a Foreign Language

Air signs are all about the exchange of information. It's important to them that they be able to get the word out and share their thoughts with others. Talking with new people helps you feel revitalized, so expand your communication skills by learning a foreign language. Try taking a course at your local community college or checking out one of the many apps and online programs to help you develop your skills. You may even consider planning a trip to the country that speaks that language. You'll get first-hand experience practicing your new skills and likely make new friends in the process!

Dive Into the Words
of a Fellow Libra

A s a generous and social sign, Libra is always busy helping others. While your compassionate nature is part of what makes you wonderful, it is also important to make the time to tend to your own needs. Nurture your intellectual side and reconnect with your celestial roots by enjoying a thought-provoking book by a fellow Libran. Try a work by one of the many great Libra authors: F. Scott Fitzgerald, Anne Rice, or Philip Pullman. You can also get your diplomatic wheels turning with a biography on an influential Libra political figure such as Eleanor Roosevelt or Margaret Thatcher.

Head Out on an Adventure

Air signs have an adventurous side, and you're known among your friends for being fun and spontaneous. If you're feeling a little bored lately, seek out some new experiences to recharge yourself and give you the excitement you need. Go for something a little unexpected with some wild (but still air-themed!) fun. Take a ride in a hot-air balloon to view your home from an entirely new perspective. Take a class to learn how to swing high on a trapeze for a unique workout. Or head out for a weekend away from home to learn kitesurfing from an expert. Give yourself the boost you need to keep your energy up!

Create a Love Potion

Oh, how Libra does *love* love! As a relationship-oriented sign, Libra feels balanced and happy when his relationships are flourishing. Feeling stuck in a romantic rut? Having trouble with a friend? Revitalize your love life with a special potion!

You can make your own love potion with the following simple recipe! Just mix 1 cup milk with 2 teaspoons honey in a small pot over medium heat. Then think of what you desire as you add in ½ teaspoon ground coriander, 3 drops vanilla extract, and 1 drop rose flavoring. Stir the ingredients until they are hot but not boiling, then pour into a wide cup and drink as you meditate once again on the love you seek.

Establish a Sleep Routine

Sleep is important to Libra's well-being, as it brings him back into balance after each busy day. If stress or illness upsets his sleep routine, he'll feel unbalanced, which can lead to a lack of confidence, and an inability to make even small decisions. Create a sleep routine in order to avoid this lack of balance. Try different aids, like yoga poses and soothing music, to find what works best for you. You should also set a consistent bedtime and time that you want to wake up so your body will adapt to fall asleep and wake up at those times.

Take a Deep Breath

———————

A ir signs have highly tuned nervous systems, so certain breathing exercises can help you stay calm and relaxed. For a simple breathing technique you can employ anywhere, start by counting up from one to ten on an exhale. Then try counting down from ten to one as you inhale. You may find it helpful to close your eyes or put your hands on your stomach or chest to feel yourself breathing. Check out online resources or apps for alternate techniques. Whenever you're feeling a little stressed, take a moment to focus on yourself and your breathing.

Avoid Negative Conversation Overload

A ir signs are social and love to talk with other people. Since words are so important to them, air signs are also great at listening. But remember this: don't let yourself get burned out by tuning into negative conversations that don't involve you. Air signs can pick up other people's vibrations and energies through words, which can sometimes lead to a mental overload. Take a break and step away from the conversation, head outside for some fresh air, or redirect your focus toward something less draining and more relevant for you.

Restore Romance with
Strawberry Begonias

A sophisticated plant with wide, red-hued leaves
and soft light-pink flowers, strawberry begonias
are the perfect addition to Libra's home. Pink is a
Libran power color, provoking his warm, loving nature.
If an imbalance has caused you to lose that loving
feeling, or you want to set the mood for a romantic
night, give your begonia plant a little extra care.
Water it, trim away dead leaves, or add a bit of liquid
fertilizer to the soil. You'll be feeling the love in no time.

Keep Your Windows Open

Your home should be a place for you to relax, recharge, and reconnect with yourself. So make sure to pay homage to your air sign qualities in your home décor. Whether you live in a house or apartment, you'll be happiest and most comfortable with lots of windows that open. Try to keep your windows open all year long, especially after a cold spell or heat wave. Even if you have central air or heat, it can be helpful to keep just one window open. Changing the air currents changes the energy in your home, so be sure to let fresh air and positive energy flow throughout your living space.

Repeat Your Mantra

The perfect mantra for Libra is "We balance our-selves and each other." Symbolized by the Scales, Libra is all about creating balance in all things, especially his relationships with others. It's important for everyone around Libra to be balanced in order for him himself to feel the same way, and as a giving sign, he is naturally more than willing to help out. This can lead Libra to focus all of his energy on the needs of others, neglecting his own necessities. In the end he may feel like his friends and family members are balanced, but he will also feel burned out and unsteady himself.

This mantra will serve as your reminder that it is not your sole responsibility to balance everyone. Other people are perfectly capable of helping themselves, and they can also help you find your own equilibrium—if you let them.

Read a Book

_____

Air signs love learning, communication, and the written word, so it makes sense that they'd also be interested in reading. If there's a book you've been dying to read or a magazine article that caught your eye, take some time for yourself and spend it reading, even if you only get to finish a couple of pages.

Not sure what you want to read? Head to your local library to check out some of the selections there. Look for a well-known classic like *Don Quixote* by Cervantes (a fellow air sign!), or try something brand-new and trendy. Still not sure where to start? Ask your librarian for a recommendation and start a conversation about some awesome books!

Socialize Responsibly

Charming Libra loves to socialize, but this can sometimes lead to overindulgence and late nights. In order to stay in balance, it's important for Libra to mind those late nights and take care to not eat or drink too much at gatherings.

If you can, ask a trusted friend or partner to help you keep track of your tendencies, or set a limit ahead of time that you know will satisfy your needs and still allow you to wake up the next morning well rested and energized. Responsibility and fun aren't necessarily mutually exclusive!

Enjoy Some Green Tea

———————

Air signs are curious and great at solving problems—but that can also mean that they're chronic overthinkers as well. Give yourself a restorative break to clear your mind and reframe your mind-set. Not sure how to begin? Try making it a habit to drink a peaceful cup of green tea every day; mix it up with some fruit-flavored or jasmine green teas for a little variety. Use your daily cup of tea as a chance to clear your mind and take a break from worrying about anything stressful in your life. (If you have health problems or are on medication, check with your doctor first.)

Afterward, you're sure to find you feel more relaxed and rejuvenated, and ready to take on any challenges that come your way. Bring your tea outside for the added benefit of a little fresh air on your break!

Prepare a Meal for Family and Friends

The ritual of meal preparation blends Libra's love of being social with putting together something beautiful. Invite your friends and family members over for a night of food and conversation, and prepare a dish that is sure to wow. Try a recipe with lots of different colors, such as a golden-brown chicken with a medley of grilled red, yellow, green, and orange vegetables.

Find an antique or modern chic tablecloth and matching napkins to really dress up your delicious spread. Also, be sure to set out two candlesticks and an even number of chairs to balance the room.

Dine Alfresco

———————

Remember, fresh air is vital for air signs, so it's important to reclaim that outdoor time for yourself. Free-spirited air signs appreciate a little spontaneous fun; try to be creative about how you find that time. For example, why not eat outdoors? Whether you're spending the day at the beach or boardwalk, or going on a picnic in the park, enjoying a healthy meal outdoors can be great for your physical and mental well-being. If you don't have time for an all-day event, you can still head outdoors by asking to be seated outside at a restaurant or even bringing a home-cooked meal out onto your own patio or deck.

Nurture Your True Self

———————

While glamour is important to Libra (given that Venus is his planetary ruler), it's also vital to maintain a balance between material and inner beauty, and avoid becoming too focused on what others think of you. Practice self-care habits that are focused solely on you, and not on impressing others. Don't worry, you don't have to go crazy with it—try dipping your toes in with a couple of small adjustments. If you typically wear makeup, or cologne, try going one or two days each week without it. Reveal your true face and scent!

This can also mean tossing pride to the wind in exchange for something others may not understand. If there's a shirt or sweater in your closet you really like, but have been reluctant to wear because it isn't "in style," pull it out and go for a walk!

Grow Purifying Houseplants

_____

Did you know that plants can help purify the air around you? Try bringing some houseplants into your home to help improve the air quality. English ivy, bamboo palm, and peace lilies are all beautiful houseplants that will help remove airborne toxins from your home. There are plenty of other options, however, so do some research to see what will grow well in your home. Warning, though, some plants are poisonous to house pets, so make sure to take the needs of your furry friends into consideration as well. Choose the plants that work best for you, and, as an air sign, you will feel your best and most balanced around these natural air purifiers.

Visit a Therapist

Big-hearted (a.k.a. relationship specialist) Libra often spends a lot of his time listening to and helping others with their problems. While it is great to provide someone else with an outlet for venting their current worries or frustrations, it's important for Libra to have an outlet of his own. Visiting a therapist, even just once every few weeks, is the perfect way to release any fear or stress you may currently be carrying. Ask your doctor for a recommendation.

It is easy for Libra to become emotionally invested in someone, so he should be aware while choosing an expert to work with that if a therapist becomes too casual and friendly with him, he will become focused on saying and doing the "correct" things in order to please them. The right therapist, however, will be an objective sounding board for Libra's problems.

Host a Game Night

Air signs love to be social, and that social interaction is all they need to spark some happiness and excitement into their everyday lives! You're likely well known for being great company, so grab some snacks, pull out your favorite games, and invite some friends over for game night! Some friendly competition and interesting conversations will help you reconnect with friends you haven't seen in a while.

For some added air sign fun, look for word-based games that will play to your language-loving strengths. Scrabble, Boggle, and Bananagrams are all popular options, but there are plenty of lesser known variations that you might enjoy.

Balance Your Emotions with Opal

Ruled by passionate Venus, Libra is a sensual, romantic sign—though his emotional side is sometimes ignored in favor of logic and diplomatic thinking. The opal is the perfect gem for balancing your quest for justice and harmony with your need for emotional expression and love. Opal has long been associated with romance and passion. As a reflective and somewhat soft gemstone, it can both absorb and express emotion, releasing any inhibitions or stabilizing intense feelings.

Do you feel daring? Black opals are a more dramatic take on the traditional milky-white color. You'll balance your emotional and logical sides—and turn heads while doing so.

Keep Communication Open

E ven great communicators like air signs can have disagreements with friends and family members. But you're likely to feel unbalanced when conflict causes the lines of communication to be closed. So clear the air and reopen those lines. It's important to remember not to hold onto grudges, so if you have any negative feelings, try to let them go and approach the conversation with a positive attitude. Do your best to be patient and flexible with the other person—remember, not everyone is as good at expression as you are! Work together to get back in balance and bring your relationships to a happier state.

Treat Yourself to a Cleaning Service

Libra has many talents, but housekeeping is not one of them. With so many people to visit and places to be, who has time to stop and clean? Hire a housekeeper or a cleaning service for your home or apartment. Even a once-monthly deep cleaning by a professional will be a weight off your shoulders, so you can relax and focus on more exciting things. Clean and decluttered, your home will have plenty of newfound space for creativity and relaxation.

Take Yourself to the Movies

Air signs love learning about new ideas, and a great way to do so is to head to the movies. Treat yourself to a couple of hours of comfortable seating, buttery popcorn, and an interesting new movie. You might try checking out a documentary or something that's particularly thought-provoking.

Although it's always fun to bring friends to the movie theater, you might consider making the occasional trip alone. Air signs appreciate the opportunity to think deeply about things they've learned. Enjoy the time alone to really analyze and fully process the movie you've just seen.

Take a Walk Near Water

Feeling unbalanced? A walk alongside a body of water is the perfect way to re-center your energy and release stress. This simple act of self-care creates a great balance between the land and the water, which is music to Libran ears.

This activity will also allow you to get some fresh air, leaving you rejuvenated and ready for anything. Try walking alongside a flowing river or standing near a waterfall if you can find one. It's the perfect balance for Libra: beauty and motion.

Hang Out in a Hammock

As an air sign, it's important for you to get outside and get some fresh air. One great way to unwind and recharge outside is to relax in a hammock. Enjoy rocking in the breeze, and give yourself permission to take a quick mental break. You can chat with friends nearby or spend some time by yourself, appreciating the nature around you. You should even feel free to close your eyes and take a little nap—you'll feel incredibly relaxed when you wake up! But if you're still in need of some mental stimulation to distract yourself, bring a book with you and take a little time to read. Your intellectual side will thank you!

Clear Space in Your Home

_____

Air signs may seem like they're in constant motion. And that's certainly true of their minds, which are often off and running to solve whatever problems come their way. Yet sometimes air signs can get thrown off—both physically and mentally—by stagnant air in their home.

If you start feeling stuck or out of balance, get rid of anything old or musty in your home or apartment. Also consider rearranging the furniture, as moving furniture allows the air to circulate more easily through your living spaces. Your thoughts will mimic the newly refreshed space and be able to flow more freely.

Accept Your Role As a Leader

While Libra may be seen as a mediator, seeking peace between everyone, his quest for harmony actually makes him a strong team leader. Don't let your ability to see both sides stop you from taking the lead. Use your ability to your advantage. Libra is known as the steel hand in a velvet glove. There is grit in this charming sign, so others should not be fooled.

Practice taking the reins on solving a small problem between friends or at work. Follow your gut instinct, and then apply your diplomacy skills to lead the group to a solution. In taking these small steps, you can work your way up to a larger leadership role.

Breathe Deeply for Balance

Libra is the sign of harmony, but it's important to not lose yourself in your romantic pursuits and partnerships. In fact, this tendency for Libra to try to please others at the expense of his own desires creates a lack of true harmony. Use a breathing exercise to step back from a situation where you may be headed toward this imbalance. Pausing to take a few deep breaths will allow you to refocus your attention to a more balanced goal for both your needs and the other person's needs.

Analyze Your Handwriting

With the air signs' interest in communication, they're likely to appreciate the importance of writing and may be very interested in what they can learn from their own handwriting. Your handwriting could be an important key to revealing some interesting aspects of your personality. Things like the slant, size, and thickness of your letters can be important, so have your handwriting analyzed! For instance, did you know that large letters indicate a big personality? If your handwriting slants to the right, you might like to meet new people. Learn some basic handwriting analysis tricks and practice your new skills with your friends to see if you can get to know them better!

Embrace Your Romantic Side

Ruled by Venus, Libra is the sign of romance, so be sure to share the affection! Leave a love note in your partner's pocket. Wear a locket with a special person's picture inside. Or show the love on a larger scale: on Valentine's Day send valentines to everyone you know. Not only will you be nourishing your own loving side, but you will also be deepening your bond with those around you. Plus, a little romance goes a long way in keeping your relationships balanced—the ultimate goal of diplomatic Libra.

Travel the World

Air signs may seem as if they're always on the move, so think about places you might like to visit to actually get yourself moving. It's always a good idea to have a trip planned for the near future. You don't have to go far or plan an extensive, expensive vacation, but a nice weekend away or a few nights in a place you've always wanted to visit can give you something to look forward to and keep your energy high. Try visiting someplace peaceful to give yourself a chance to recharge, or research places you could visit to add an intellectual element to your next trip, like cities with interesting museums or historical monuments. Your adventurous free spirit will appreciate the change of scenery.

Continue Your Education

Air signs are the intellectuals of the zodiac and are always looking to learn something new. Continue your education by pursuing an advanced degree. By doing so, you'll be practicing good mental self-care through fully engaging in an intellectual pursuit. However, you might also find some practical benefits to continuing your education. By pursuing a degree in your field, you may discover that you're better qualified for a different position in your company. Or, if you choose to expand your horizons and go for a new degree in an entirely different field, you might be able to move into a new dream job.

Take Someone
Ballroom Dancing

B allroom dancing is the perfect blend of exercising and spending quality time with your partner. As an air sign, Libra will love the fluid movements of the dance, while his need for strong, harmonious relationships will be fulfilled by the intimate experience. As you and your partner move in harmony to the music, you'll feel your connection deepening—not to mention all of the great memories you'll be making together!

Ballroom dancing is also a balancing act, using complementary steps to create a passionate presentation. If you have the space to dance in your own home, try a flirtatious fox-trot to Frank Sinatra's "I've Got You Under My Skin," or a passionate tango to Carlos Gardel's "Amargura."

Stop Gossiping

Because air signs are so great at communication, people really enjoy talking to them. That can be great news—you love speaking to and learning from a lot of people—but you need to be careful with everything you learn. People will often feel comfortable sharing their personal issues with you, and it's up to you to be respectful of that. Avoid gossiping, and don't share anyone's personal information without their permission. For someone as social as you are, it's important that you keep your friendships in good shape. Your friends trust you, so remember to honor their feelings to keep your relationships going strong.

Lie Out in an Open Field

Libra loves open spaces, as he has a touch of claustrophobia due to his air element. Take a trip out to an open field where you can lie down, either on a blanket or directly on the grass, and soak in the fresh air. Take deep breaths in and out to establish balance. Enjoy the harmony of nature in its blended colors and sounds. Give yourself time to daydream. A simple act of self-care, this trip into nature is just the thing to recharge your batteries for your next adventure.

Decorate with Wind Chimes

Air signs can sometimes have the energy of a powerful wind with their free-spirited natures. Why not bring that inspiration into your home décor? Try putting some wind chimes on your porch, by the entrance to your home, or somewhere else where you'll be able to hear them often. If you live in an apartment, putting your chimes near a window should be enough to get them ringing.

Putting a wind chime in your home can be a great way to remind yourself of some of your great air sign qualities. Every time you hear it ringing, you'll be reminded of your fun, adventurous side!

Drink Plenty of Water

L ibra rules over the kidneys. The kidneys are an important part of your overall health. These small powerhouses work to remove toxins and other waste from your blood before it is pumped up to your heart. In order to promote proper kidney function, you should make sure you're drinking the recommended amount of water each day (depending on sex, lifestyle, climate, and health). Drink up, Libra!

Sign Up for a Writing Course

Air signs are known for being great at expression and deep thinking. So why not expand your communication skills by taking a writing course? Although it may seem intimidating to put all your thoughts onto paper, you may be surprised to find you have a hidden writing talent! The good news is, writing classes span a variety of areas from fiction and poetry to screenwriting and presentation development. You're sure to find something that fits your interests!

You may find that you thrive in a social environment, like a class at a local college, where you can share your ideas with your classmates and develop your skills together. But if you're feeling a little shy about sharing your first writing attempts in person, there are plenty of online courses you can explore to get started.

Strike the Extended Triangle Pose

The Extended Triangle Pose is perfect for Libra as it promotes balance, which is essential to his well-being. To do this pose, stand up straight with your arms at your sides. Next, slide your feet out to the sides until they are 3–4 metric feet apart. Raise your arms out to the sides, palms facing down. Next, turn your left foot just slightly to the right and your right foot to the right a full 90 degrees. Inhale, then, as you start to exhale, bend at your hip to the right. Place your right hand on your shin, ankle, or the floor, and extend your left arm toward the ceiling. Turn your gaze upward to your left hand (if it feels comfortable to do so). Hold this pose for five to ten breaths, then move out of it as you slowly inhale. Reverse your feet and repeat the pose on your left side.

Learn Calligraphy

If you're an air sign, you're all about communication. Get creative with your communication style and study calligraphy! Calligraphy is a beautiful writing form that can take a lot of practice to master but can also be a rewarding skill. You may be able to share your abilities for things like wedding invitations, announcements, or memorials.

Calligraphy can also be a meditative practice, giving overthinking air signs a much-needed mental break. Allow yourself time to slow down and focus on each careful, deliberate movement instead of worrying about a problem at hand. Taking a break to focus on your calligraphy will help you redirect your attention and feel refreshed.

Plan a Trip to China

China is the perfect location for a Libran holiday. Ruled by Venus, Libra has a great appreciation for beauty—especially beauty rooted in history and long-standing tradition. He easily gets swept up in the romance of a place and its people. And with China's winding Great Wall, legendary Yellow Mountain, and other breathtaking sites, there is a lot to get swept up in! Even if your trip is far off in the future, just planning this amazing experience will have you energized and in full Libran spirits.

Visit Some Butterflies

Air signs can be spontaneous and would love to head out on an airy getaway. Try visiting a butterfly sanctuary! A butterfly sanctuary is an indoor living space or conservatory designed specifically for the breeding, development, and safe display of butterflies. They also offer lots of opportunities to learn about the butterflies and the ways we can conserve and protect them!

This visit can be a great opportunity to take care of yourself physically since you can spend plenty of time walking around the garden areas. This enjoyable activity can also have emotional benefits. Your positive mood is sure to carry through into your day well after you leave the sanctuary.

Gain Confidence with Centaury

Compassionate Libra is always ready to help others. Sometimes, however, his focus on other people can lead to anxious thoughts as he tries to please everyone. A helpful flower remedy for Libra's anxiety is centaury.

Created by Edward Bach, the Bach Flower Remedies are solutions of brandy and diluted wild flower materials that retain the healing properties of that flower. Specifically, the centaury remedy helps kind, sensitive people like Libra who can become anxious in their desire to please. The Bach Flower Remedies can be used by adding a couple of drops to a glass of water and sipping slowly (follow the directions on the bottle).

Feed the Birds

All birds are friends to air signs—they share your free-spirited nature! You may find it soothing and calming to watch birds fly about. Why not encourage them to come to your yard by setting up a bird feeder? Different birds will like different foods, so try putting out a seed mix, suet, or even the popular black oil sunflower seed that attracts many different kinds of birds. Make sure to place your feeder in a safe place away from predators and windows. You may even want to get expert advice on adopting (and properly caring for) a parakeet, mynah bird, or canary as a pet from a local animal shelter!

Get a Massage

Soothing healing practices like massage are very Venusian—perfect for Venus-ruled Libra. The sensual experience of pressure on your muscles and joints, especially when coupled with the heat of stones or oil, is heavenly. Have the masseuse focus on your lower back, which can be a problematic area for Libra. For ultimate relaxation, be sure to select a location that is aesthetically pleasing. A spa that is undergoing renovations or is beside a building eyesore will affect your ability to completely focus on your massage.

Enjoy the Morning Crossword

Sometimes, doing something to keep your mind sharp is an important way to take care of yourself. Successfully completing a challenging task can help you feel stimulated and ready to take on the next project that comes your way. For air signs who love language and are often great problem-solvers, a crossword puzzle is a great way to exercise your mind. A word puzzle also has the added benefit of helping you learn new vocabulary, which air signs will love. Establish a new daily ritual and try doing your crossword puzzle in the morning—your success will help set the positive tone for the rest of the day!

Nurture Your Nervous System with Figs

Figs are high in calcium and potassium, which promote a healthy nervous system. Air signs like Libra have especially sensitive nervous systems, so it is important to give special care to this part of your body.

Figs are also a delicious treat that is ruled by Libra's sensual planet, Venus. A few bites will have you feeling like a divine god or goddess yourself. You can enjoy them in fresh slices, or mix them into a green salad for a burst of color and nutrition!

Attend an Interesting Lecture

Air signs are naturally curious and love learning, so try attending a lecture or other form of presentation. Keep it fun and interesting by attending lectures on subjects that pique your curiosity. You may even be able to find presentations by popular speakers for free through your local library or other organizations in your area. Take some time for yourself to learn something new!

Doing something mentally stimulating will put all air signs in a good mood, but attending a lecture can also have an added social benefit. You may find yourself making friends with your fellow attendees as you discuss your shared interests after the event is over.

Window-Shop at Fancy Locations

_____

Feeling a little less upbeat than your usual bubbly self? Go window-shopping. As a sign ruled by the alluring planet Venus, Libra has a deep appreciation for beauty. A trip to a charming shopping mall or sophisticated store is the perfect boost of positive energy. You don't need to buy anything to feel the uplifting effects (though you certainly can if you want to). Just window-shopping in a beautiful place is therapeutic for luxe-loving Libra.

Think Through Your Decisions

Air signs are great at critical thinking and like to make logical decisions. They'd rather follow their heads than let their emotions get in the way of their decision-making. Yet, because air signs like to take their time to see all sides of a question, making big decisions can prove difficult.

The best advice here is to not let yourself get rushed or pressured into making a decision. If you're feeling unbalanced, you can get trapped thinking in and out of hundreds of potential scenarios—many of which will never occur. If this happens, remember to take care of your emotions and your body; try doing some deep breathing and allowing your intuition to help you figure out which solutions are the best for you.

Wear Pastels

Pastels are the perfect representation of Libra: welcoming and oh-so beautiful. Soft yellow, blue, and pink shades create a stylish and elegant look that Venus-ruled Libra will love showing off at his next party. Pastels also provide a fresh, airy vibe for this air sign.

Be sure to choose the right color for each occasion. Yellow and pink are perfect for an energizing afternoon of fun with friends, while blue works best when you are looking to relax or encourage communication within your relationships.

Clear Your Mind with Meditation

We've all heard about the many benefits of meditation: it can reduce stress, depression, and anxiety; increase happiness, focus, and self-awareness; and even improve your physical health. Some research has indicated that meditation can be helpful for everything from minor aches and pains and even the simple headache to major illnesses—including asthma, chronic pain, heart conditions, and cancer. Meditation is a perfect activity for air signs, who can use it to find balance and harmony in their everyday lives.

Use your meditation practice as an opportunity to redirect your attention. Meditation will allow you to clear your mind and breathe, so you'll stay emotionally and physically healthy.

Practice Tai Chi

Tai chi, short for *Tàijíquán*, is a martial arts practice focused on fluid movements and breathing. As an air sign, Libra needs to incorporate graceful motions and deep breathing into his self-care routine. Tai chi is also deeply rooted in the philosophy of balance, something that Libra places great value on. In fact, the term *taiji* in *Tàijíquán* refers to yin and yang: the opposing forces of the universe that together create balance. Tai chi incorporates these forces into its moves.

Tai chi has also evolved into a seated exercise that you can use to reduce and manage stress. Described as "meditation in motion," this modern form of tai chi promotes calm through modified elegant, flowing movements. You can find countless tai chi lessons and routines online!

Celebrate Your Alone Time

_____

A ir signs are very social, and are known for being great company because they can keep any situation from becoming too boring. However, it's important that you don't let yourself get burned out by spending all your time keeping other people entertained. It's good to take some time for yourself! Appreciate the time you have to spend doing something you like, whether that's heading outdoors or learning something new. Taking time to concentrate on yourself will give you a positive outlook and a fresh perspective. So instead of always focusing on others, reframe your mind-set and simply enjoy being alone.

Try Next-Level Yoga

Beyond individual poses, Libra should pursue more advanced yoga to further his internal balance. Try hot yoga, a modern form of yoga class that is performed in a heated room. The heat helps prepare the body for movement by warming up the muscles. Additionally, the poses used in hot yoga are often a bit more advanced than in traditional yoga. One popular form of hot yoga you can find in many locations is Bikram Yoga. Bikram Yoga incorporates a heated room with twenty-six poses and two breathing exercises.

Look out for local beginners' classes. Be sure to hydrate your body beforehand and to bring a water bottle and small towel with you to class.

Subscribe to New Podcasts

There are all kinds of ways to learn new information, and air signs are especially good at learning by listening. A great way for you to gather more information might be through podcasts. Podcasts are perfect for when you're on the go, since you can listen wherever you are, whether you're driving, grocery shopping, or even working out. There's a lot to learn, so choose a topic that you find interesting and simply search for the right podcast for you!

Listening to a podcast can also be a nice mental break. Centering your thoughts on whatever you're listening to can help you relax and redirect your mind away from any problem that's worrying you.

Boost Your Creativity
with "Imagine"

L ibra is one of the most imaginative signs of the zodiac. Ruled by Venus, he has a special connection to the five senses, which enables him to envision (and create) amazing things. But, sometimes, even the most creative Libra could use a little extra inspiration. Play "Imagine" by fellow Libran John Lennon when you need a spark to ignite your next big idea, or more fuel to finish your current project. The soothing rhythm will also act as an opposing force to your vigorous energy, providing more balance to your day.

Cleanse Your Home by Smoke Cleansing

The state of your mind is often reflected in the state of your home. If there's clutter everywhere and dust is starting to gather, there's a good chance you're feeling stuck emotionally and mentally as well. For intellectual air signs, this clutter can make you feel unbalanced and distressed. Smoke cleansing is a simple ritual that you can use to clear out negativity in your home (and also your mind!) and inspire a fresh, positive start.

All you'll need to get started is a bundle of rosemary, a fireproof bowl, and some matches or a lighter. Tidy up any obvious clutter and open as many doors and windows as possible in your home. Place the rosemary in a fireproof bowl and light the bundle. Blow it out and use the fireproof bowl to hold the smoking bundle as you walk around your home, spreading the smoke throughout and focusing on its ability to remove negativity. Make way for a refreshed, positive attitude!

Splurge on a Haircut or Facial

A motivating factor for Libra in self-care is pride in his appearance. When the reflection in the mirror looks healthy and well rested, Libra feels good. Take care of your lovely looks by treating yourself to a haircut or facial, or both. The sensual experience of having your mane shampooed and trimmed, or your skin released of built-up oil and dirt, is hard to beat. Plus, when you walk out the door with a stylish new do and luminous skin, heads are sure to turn.

Perform Random Acts
of Kindness

Air signs can be extremely thoughtful; they're great at being objective when they need to be and genuinely want to see positive changes in the world around them. An easy way for air signs to help make a small change every day is to complete a random act of kindness. This can be anything from adding some extra coins to a parking meter that's about to run out to volunteering for a good cause. You could also pay for your coworker's coffee when you see them in the drive-thru line behind you, pack your partner's lunch for the day, or call an elderly relative just to chat about their week.

Making simple acts of kindness a daily ritual can strengthen your relationships by showing others how much you care about them, and can improve your own everyday outlook!

Balance Your Checkbook

L ibra likes nice things, which can come with not-so-nice price tags. Keep your finances in order so that your earnings and spending are in balance. This could mean balancing your checkbook after each transaction, or designating one day each week (or month) to going over your finances and tracking them with a spreadsheet or other detailed document. There are also many phone apps available that can sync with your credit and debit cards and automatically categorize how you are spending your money.

Enjoy a Rainy Day

Air signs are connected to the weather—after all, your mood can change just as quickly and drastically as the winds! Take some time to connect with and appreciate changes in the weather instead of letting them get you down. Don't let yourself get upset by a rainy day. Instead, enjoy a good rainstorm! Sit by your window and simply savor the wind and rain. You may find it helps you relax to bring a cup of tea with you or take a few deep, meditative breaths. By training yourself to look at things in a positive light, you'll take better care of your emotional needs and feel happier every day.

Donate Unused Items

A lover of the latest trends in clothing and home accessories, Libra can easily end up with a stockpile of things that end up collecting dust. Devote a day to sorting through all of these possessions and donating the items that you don't use. You may think that you'll someday need that dusty exercise bike, but if you haven't used it in the last few months, you most likely never will.

Decluttering your space can help reduce stress, while releasing some of the material possessions that may be weighing you down more than you think.

Balance Your Mind and Body
with Pilates

E ven though air signs are often focused on the
mind, it's just as important to take care of the body
through exercise. The secret to consistent exercise?
Find a workout routine that works for you and that
you enjoy! Not only will your body feel healthy and
strong, but you'll also head into your workout with a
much more positive attitude.

· One routine that might work well for air signs is a
Pilates class, which focuses on both the mind and the
body as you work your way through different moves.
You'll learn to strengthen your physique through careful movement, develop your flexibility and balance,
and properly manage your breathing for less stress
and more control of your body.

Volunteer for a
Social Justice Cause

S ymbolized by the Scales, Libra is passionate about fairness for all. Find a cause that allows you to bring more fairness to the world. Social justice movements that you can join include everything from gender equality to access to education. You can march at a local rally, work at a fundraiser, or spread the word about a great cause. As the astrological diplomat, you have the ability to see a perspective and express it clearly to others—so use it. Your voice can make the difference, Libra!

Take Care of Yourself

If you're an air sign, you know you can sometimes get trapped in your own head. Air signs are intellectual people, which makes them great problem-solvers and critical thinkers. However, there's always the risk of overthinking and spending too much time living in your mind. Don't let yourself get too detached from daily life!

Completing necessary, practical activities is essential self-care. Things like eating three good meals a day, showering, and brushing your teeth every morning and evening are important for keeping your life in balance. So remember to stay grounded in the real world and do the things you need to do to keep yourself healthy and happy.

Sip a Cup of Chamomile

Always on the go and meeting new people, Libra needs to be well rested. Ready to wind down but feeling a bit too energized after the excitement of the past day? Try having a cup of chamomile tea! In fact, Libra should make this a regular bedtime ritual! Soothing and subtly sweet, chamomile tea is a wonderful natural sleep aid. (If you suffer from plant allergies or are on medication, check with your doctor first.) You will be drifting off to dreamland in no time.

Create a Bright, Open Home

A ir signs are always on the move and can seem
a little restless. So it's important that you use
your home space as a place to restore and refocus.
Create a beautiful, air-friendly home where you'll feel
comfortable and able to relax.

Your design aesthetic is likely to be light, open,
and airy. To start, don't set up your living spaces with
so many components that they feel overcomplicated—
simple spaces are important to air signs! Also, take
some time to think about the lighting for your home.
All the lights in your home should be full spectrum,
which will help imitate the sunny outdoors, even on
the rainiest days.

Feel Grounded
with Free Weights

A s an air sign, Libra often has his head in the clouds. While big ideas and lighthearted fun are part of what makes him wonderful, Libra should also make time to re-ground himself in reality once in a while. Lifting weights is a great exercise for keeping your feet firmly planted on the ground and your senses focused on the here and now. Ask your fitness trainer for weight and technique guidance.

Weight lifting is also a great way to release stress and decompress after a busy day. As you focus on strengthening your muscles, any tension you feel will slowly release with each movement. There's also the added bonus that you'll look great after doing it!

Buy a Pair of Leather Driving Gloves

If there is one thing Libra knows, it's how to do everything with a touch of class. Leather driving gloves may not be necessary in the modern vehicle, but they are certainly sophisticated. Ruled by Venus, Libra will especially love the smooth, somewhat daring feel of leather (real or fake).

One thing people may not realize is that Libra also has a tough side and has an urge to drive in the fast lane. Sure, you are a gentle sign with a knack for making others feel at home, but you also know how to get down to business. Slip on your gloves and go for a whirl—just be sure to keep to the speed limit and buckle up first.

Have a Good Laugh

S ocial air signs love to have a good time with their friends and family. Look for ways you can enjoy a laugh together! While the emotional and social benefits of sharing a laugh are clear, did you know laughter can also help your physical health by decreasing stress, lowering blood pressure, relieving pain, and even boosting your immune system? Taking some time to laugh every day will have a wide range of restorative benefits.

All you need to do is head to a comedy club or watch a silly movie. Or keep a book of puns, jokes, and limericks handy for when you need a pick-me-up or a reason to share a giggle with other people. Your love of language will make it doubly enjoyable for you!

Ease Overactive Thoughts
with St. John's Wort

———————

Libra cares deeply about his relationships. In fact, part of the Libra identity is tied into balance within his family, friendship circle, and romantic connections. Sometimes, Libra can get caught up in trying to make everyone happy, leaving him feeling overwhelmed and out of balance himself. St. John's wort is a natural supplement that may help calm the anxious thoughts that Libra sometimes experiences. Talk to your doctor to ask if it may help you (St. John's wort is not suitable for everyone and can interact with other medications), as well as to discuss specific dosing recommendations.

Invest in an Air Purifier

A s an air sign, you know that the quality of the air around you is important for your health and well-being. Clean air is especially important for your physical health, but the truth is that everyone can benefit! Keeping dust, smog, and other tiny particles out of your lungs is an important way to not only keep you feeling your best, but also helps prevent other serious illnesses. Research and invest in a good air purifier to help eliminate things like pollen, smoke, or other pollutants from the air in your home. An air purifier can be especially important if you live in a city where the increased population and traffic can mean more pollution.

Playact

I gnite your creativity and give yourself a confidence boost with a little playacting. It may seem counterproductive, but sometimes the best way for Libra to feel like himself is by pretending to be someone else. The time-out from his own thoughts and feelings is the perfect way to recharge and gain some perspective.

Step into someone else's shoes for the afternoon: dress in a way you normally wouldn't dress; try out personality traits that don't come as naturally to you. At the end of the "show," you'll return to yourself with a creative reminder of all of the things that make you amazing.

Decorate with Clear Quartz

Crystals can be a great way to add some beauty to a space and help rebalance your energy. Air signs will find lots of benefits from clear quartz crystals, which are among the most common and well-known healing stones. Learn about ways quartz may help treat you physically (crystal healing with clear quartz can be useful for the nervous system!) and mentally. Since clear quartz is believed to increase spiritual connections and clear thinking, it can be a useful tool when you need to expand your thoughts and think carefully.

Try decorating your home and office space with clear quartz crystal clusters so there's always one nearby when you start to feel a little off-balance.

Plant Morning Glories

Few appreciate beauty quite like Libra does. Ruled by Venus, he has a keen eye for aesthetics, particularly the grace and class of a flawless floral arrangement and striking outdoor blossoms. Morning glories are a perfect vine to accent the Libran home. This traditional flower will evoke a sophisticated atmosphere, while the soft blue color of the petals promotes calm and communication. Consider using morning glory blooms as a centerpiece in your living or dining room, where they are sure to impress your guests and encourage open, relaxed conversation.

Listen to Conversation Around You

A ir signs are the element of communication, so it's only natural for you to pay attention to the conversations around you. You're also always ready to learn new things, so you're likely to be listening for subjects that might pique your interest. Whether you're riding the subway, waiting in line at the supermarket, or mingling at a party, you're sure to catch some snippets of chatter that grab your attention. You might even consider carrying around a notebook and pen to jot down little bits of conversation you hear or interesting topics you'd like to learn more about later.

Bring On the Kiwifruit

Having trouble sleeping? Airy Libra can be quite the tornado of energy, which is great for a productive day, but not so great come bedtime. Don't fret; simply add more kiwi to your diet! Kiwifruit contains a number of powerful compounds, including serotonin, which is an important chemical in sleep regulation.

Kiwifruit is also loaded with vitamins and minerals, such as vitamins B_6 and B_{12} and magnesium. These vitamins and minerals are key in relieving and managing stress. Plus kiwi is a delicious, colorful treat, perfect for topping frozen yogurt or salad, or enjoying by itself.

Choose Light, Fresh Scents

Air signs find it helpful for their living spaces to be well lit and spacious to mimic the natural world. So it makes sense that you'd also prefer lighter, more natural scents for your home. Whether you're looking for candles, room sprays, or other scented products, choose light scents like lemon verbena and rosewater. Even if you typically hate perfumes or colognes, these scents aren't overpowering. Instead, they'll make the air smell fresh and clean, which will help you feel more relaxed and at home in your living space. Certain scents also come with plenty of other benefits—for instance, a citrusy smell can help you feel a bit more energized!

Try Feng Shui

It's important to get a good night's sleep so you wake up feeling enlivened and reinvigorated. For air signs, sleep is also an important aspect of keeping your nervous system in balance. Use the power of some basic feng shui to help you get exactly the right setup for better rest.

Feng shui is the practice of aligning and arranging elements in your home to create the ideal energy flow for positivity and good luck in various aspects of your life. To improve sleep, you should avoid positioning the bed so your feet point toward the bedroom door, which can decrease your personal energy. Considering things like the way other furniture in your bedroom can impede the flow of energy can also be helpful to improve your sleep.

Attract Romance with a Pink Candle

Ruled by the sensual planet Venus, Libra is the sign of love. Looking for someone to shower your Libran affection on? Light a pink candle to draw romance into your life. The soft, sensual color of the candle represents love, while the act of burning candles is crucial in spellcasting traditions.

To complete this ritual, light the candle and let it burn down fully while you are in the room. As it burns, visualize yourself receiving the love you desire.

Learn about the Weather

Air signs are sensitive to changes in the weather, so you're already likely to be very aware of the changes in the air around you. You can encourage your intellectual interests and take better care of your physical self by learning a little more about the weather. Purchase an old-fashioned barometer to keep in your home.

A barometer is a scientific instrument that's often used to predict the weather because it measures changes in the atmospheric pressure. High pressure usually indicates good weather, but watch out if that level starts to drop! Not only will you learn a fun new piece of information to share, you'll also be prepared no matter the weather with just a glance at your barometer.

Toast with a Grasshopper

Venusian Libra loves cocktails that offer a complete sensory experience. Combining a rich blend of tastes and aromas, as well as a striking green color, the grasshopper cocktail is the perfect Libran refreshment.

Making your own grasshopper cocktail at home is simple. In a shaker filled with ice, combine ¾ ounce cream, ¾ ounce white crème de cacao, and ¾ ounce green crème de menthe. Shake vigorously, then strain into a chilled cocktail glass. Top off the glass with a shaving of dark chocolate and voilà!

De-Stress with Kiteflying

Sometimes, acting like a kid is a great way to release stress. And what is a better throwback activity for an air sign than flying a kite! Air signs can easily get wrapped up in their own thoughts, so an activity like flying kites that gets you out into the natural world, and gives you something to take your mind off your worries, can be a big help for your stress level. If you find you really enjoy kiteflying, you might consider checking out a kiteflying competition to develop your skills even more, and make some new friends. You may even get a little exercise from chasing your kite around!

Find Balance with Ametrine

A metrine is the perfect meditation stone for Libra, due to its inherent stable nature. This eye-catching orange and purple crystal is made of a combination of amethyst and citrine. Amethyst represents spiritual enlightenment, while citrine represents physical expression and grounding joy. Ametrine's unique blend of the metaphysical plane of amethyst and the physical plane of citrine creates perfect balance. Keep this stone with you always in the form of a bracelet or ring, or use it to meditate in your home.

Go on a Weekly Hike

Air signs need to spend plenty of time out in the fresh air, so they're likely to feel reenergized after heading out for a hike. If you go out to the woods or fields, you'll get a chance to view some beautiful scenery while you walk.

You can also combine your appreciation for the outdoors with your workout schedule! Hiking is a great workout that can improve heart health, strengthen muscles, and increase stability and balance. It's also often recommended as a natural stress-relief activity. It's just as important to take care of your body as it is your mind, so add a weekly hike to your workouts!

Restore Joy with Lavender

Above everything, Libra values harmony in all things. From his relationships to his home, he seeks balance. As a compassionate sign, he tends to take on the full responsibility of creating and restoring balance for both himself and those around him, which can lead to feeling overwhelmed and run-down. If you are in need of a little release, lavender essential oil is the perfect way to ease stress and recharge your batteries.

Boasting a sweet, floral scent, lavender has a soothing effect that calms anxious thoughts and promotes relaxation, as well as a good night's sleep. You can diffuse lavender essential oil in your living or sleeping space, massage it (diluted according to instructions) onto your skin, or spritz it (diluted according to instructions) on your pillow before bed to relax.

Create a Grounding Space

With so many people to see and exciting plans in the works, Libra needs a space that allows him to touch back down to earth once in a while. Design a room in your home where you can pause and refocus before dashing off on your next adventure. Use darker colors such as indigo blue and burgundy, combined with a soft neutral like ivory or cream, to create a sense of calm and balance. Earthy accents like wood and potted plants will provide a feeling of stability.

Learn to Dance

Fluid, airy movements are aesthetically pleasing to air signs, so you may enjoy watching ballet or modern dance. If you're feeling ready to jump up and start dancing yourself, consider signing up for a class to learn more about those styles. Dance has a lot of benefits for your physical health—you can develop your strength, increase your flexibility, and improve your posture. But it can also be an effective way to relieve stress and build confidence. As you focus on learning specific steps and developing your skills, you'll have the opportunity to clear your overactive mind so you feel refreshed and ready to take on the rest of the day.

Arrange a High Tea

Sophisticated Libra knows a get-together over tea is the civilized thing to do. Not only that, but it provides the perfect setting for deep conversation with close friends. Libra places great importance on relationships, so he will appreciate the opportunity to strengthen his friendships even more.

You can set up a room in your home with all of the essentials for your classy party, or book an afternoon at a teahouse. If you do host, just be sure to bring out the fancier dishware!

Release Sky Lanterns

Create time for yourself to take care of your spiritual needs! If you've recently experienced a loss of someone from your life, it is important to honor both those people and your own feelings. Turn to your air sign–inspired appreciation for nature and call upon the energy in the air around you for some help by releasing a fire-retardant sky lantern. (Just be sure to check regulations in your area and research the safest method and locations for releasing the lanterns before doing so.) Simply write a message on the lantern to your loved one and then release it into the sky. Allowing the air, your influencing element, to carry your message where it needs to be can give you the closure and release you've been seeking.

Savor Buttercrunch Candy

Libra adores indulging his senses. Ruled by luxu-
riant Venus, he understands the healing powers
of even a small treat—especially when it comes to his
taste buds. Splurge on a box of buttercrunch candy—
or make your own at home! The rich, sugary sweet
flavors are sure to lift your spirits and encourage a
bit of relaxation. This delicious candy also makes for
a lovely surprise to share with friends and neighbors,
which generous Libra enjoys.

Keep a Loved One with You Always

For Libra an important part of happiness is close interpersonal relationships. Feeling less than your usual bubbly self? Having a picture on hand of someone you love is a simple yet effective way to brighten your mood and put you back in a positive mental space. Wear a locket with a special person's picture inside, or keep a photo tucked into your wallet where you can easily see it. Your loved ones give you strength, so keep them close!

Take Up Tennis

Take some inspiration from fellow air sign Serena Williams, and try tennis (or racquetball)! Many air signs experience bursts of energy, which work well for a sport like tennis. It's no surprise that tennis or racquetball can be great workouts that develop muscles, improve hand-eye coordination, and strengthen heart health. But as an intellectual air sign, you might also find you enjoy the tactical nature of the game. Your critical-thinking skills might help you figure out the techniques, moves, and patterns you need to win the game. Clear your mind from other thoughts and focus on keeping your movements strong and fluid.

Eat Honey

Rich and sweet, honey is the perfect indulgence for Venus-ruled Libra. But what you may not know is that, as long as you are not allergic to bees or bee products, honey is also healthy! Pure honey is full of health-promoting antioxidants that are linked to heart health. It also lowers blood pressure, improves cholesterol, soothes sore throat, and promotes healthy skin and hair.

To enjoy the benefits of honey, you can stir a little honey into your tea, or relish a spoonful straight from the jar. You can also make a rejuvenating face mask by mixing 2 teaspoons of honey with 1 teaspoon of aloe vera gel.

Decorate with Mirrors

A s an air sign, Libra needs plenty of open space for his creativity to shine. Mirrors are an easy way to make your home feel twice as big—even if home is a studio apartment with one window and a closet-sized bedroom.

Ruled by Venus, Libra also needs décor that expresses style and luxury, so your mirrors should have a touch of gilt, such as a gold frame or gold foil accents. Experiment with the mirror placement to find the best locations for ultimate openness in your space.

Keep a Journal

L ibra has so many thoughts and feelings—and so much pressure to set them aside for the sake of being amiable! Libra has a talent for making others feel relaxed and happy, but sometimes his own feelings can be lost in his quest to please everyone else. Keep a journal to write your emotions in on a daily or at least a weekly basis. While you may have the urge to swallow your feelings, this will only cause them to be bottled up until you eventually burst. Taking the time to write out all of your thoughts allows you to fully experience them, and then reflect on them. As you release them onto the page, you'll feel yourself released from their weight.

Find Balance Through Reiki

Sometimes an air sign can become unbalanced, perhaps due to overthinking or an issue with communication. When unbalanced, you may have difficulty being open-minded, and feel unwilling to accept new ideas—or you may feel overwhelmed with options. A Reiki treatment can be useful for reestablishing order in your life.

Reiki is a healing technique that aims to improve the movement of energy throughout the body through gentle touch. A Reiki session can cleanse your energy so it flows through your body smoothly and gets you back into balance. This practice will help you feel revitalized and refreshed, so be sure to consider setting up a session during high-stress times.

Make a Rejuvenating Playlist

―――――――――

L ibra is the life of the party, but even he could use an extra boost of energy once in a while. Make a playlist to get you back into the partying mood. Your playlist should include fellow Librans, such as Bruce Springsteen (his hit "Hungry Heart" may just be Libra's theme song), Bruno Mars, Gwen Stefani, Sting, and Ray Charles. Who knows how to energize a Libra better than a Libra does? So crank up the tunes and show off your dance moves!

About the Author

Constance Stellas is an astrologer of Greek heritage with more than twenty-five years of experience. She primarily practices in New York City and counsels a variety of clients, including business CEOs, artists, and scholars. She has been interviewed by *The New York Times*, *Marie Claire*, and *Working Woman*, and has appeared on several New York TV morning shows, featuring regularly on Sirius XM and other national radio programs as well. Constance is the astrologer for *HuffPost* and a regular contributor to Thrive Global. She is also the author of several titles, including *The Astrology Gift Guide*, *Advanced Astrology for Life*, *The Everything® Sex Signs Book*, and the graphic novel series Tree of Keys, as well as coauthor of *The Hidden Power of Everyday Things*. Learn more about Constance at her website, ConstanceStellas.com, or on *Twitter* (@Stellastarguide).